The last of the women chainmakers, Lucy Woodall, photogr̶ ̶ ̶ ̶ ̶ ̶ in October 1970 at the
factory of Samuel Woodhouse and Sons in Cradley Heath. L
maker in 1912. She was thirteen years old and worked from
and Sunday off. For this she received 4 shillings a week. Af
when her 'stint' was completed she could make some extra r
was 9 shillings a week. During the First World War she m
trap chains for Africa, loom chains, double twisted backbar
sort of light chain there was'. Lucy was an unusually skille
one type of chain. When visited at her home in 1978 Lucy
years at the block. However, her resilience showed through
for charity. Lucy died in 1979.

CHAINS AND
CHAINMAKING

Charles Fogg

Shire Publications Ltd

CONTENTS

Set in 10 on 9 point Times roman and printed in Great Britain by C. I. Thomas & Sons (Haverfordwest) Ltd, Press Buildings, Merlins Bridge, Haverfordwest.

Copyright © 1981 by Charles Fogg. First published 1981. Shire Album 69. ISBN 0 85263 561 3.

COVER: *Chainmakers at work shutting chain.*

BELOW: *A double twisted backband. This chain was designed to fit across the back of a horse and was made with twisted links so that it would lie flat. According to Lucy Woodall, 'You had to do all the middle first and the last link you'd shut would be a shorter link to tighten it up (1). On each end you'd put a link twisted over twice (2) to tighten the two ends before you put the end links on.'*

One of Noah Hingley's chainshops at the end of the nineteenth century. Established in 1820, this firm was the first to make a chain cable in the Black Country.

INTRODUCTION

This book is not concerned with that type of chain used for the transmission of power on motorcycles but with the kind of chain seen nevertheless every day: chain on park swings and around gardens, mooring chains on ships, chain for securing heavy loads on lorries and trains, and, at the lower end of the scale, dog chains and security chains for doors. But these instances represent only about one per cent of the total usage of this type of chain. The other ninety-nine per cent is used out of sight, in industry, mostly in the handling of materials. Industrial uses include sling and crane chains, chains for mixing materials and transmitting heat in the manufacture of cement, chains on North Sea oil rigs, conveyor chains in coal mines and chains for trawling gear in the fishing industry.

The traditional method of making such chains was very different from the way it is done today. Modern methods of manufac-turing chain on machines began in the first quarter of the twentieth century with the development of electric butt-resistance welding. The chain made on these machines was of steel rather than iron. In the early days of the electric welding machine much still depended, as in the traditional methods, on the skill of the operator. For many years the two separate sides of the industry co-existed but rapid advances in the speed and quality of production of the machine-made product caused the inevitable decline of the older industry.

The most advanced methods of making chain in the 1980s use alloys containing nickel, chrome and molybdenum. The chain is heat-treated to even out the stresses set up at the electric welding stage of the process. The finished product has high tensile strength and ductility and a very high strength-to-weight ratio. Iron

Types of chain: 1, cart trace; 2, plough trace; 3, double twisted backband; 4, hurdle shackle; 5, knotted plough trace; 6, draft chain; 7, back end; 8, fore end; 9, single twisted backband; 10, frammel ring; 11, spring billet; 12, hooks.

4

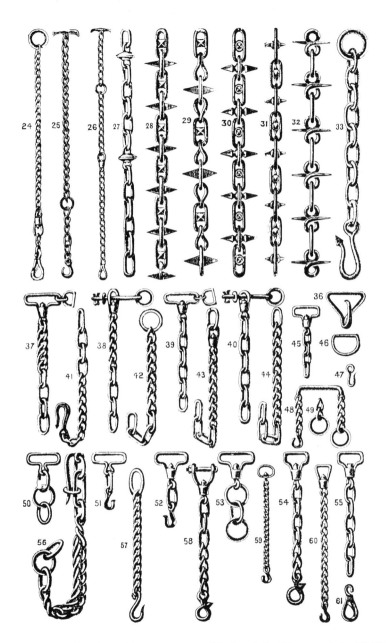

Types of chain: 24, pillar chain; 25, manger chain; 26, dog chain; 27, pump chain; 28-32, spike or fence chains; 33, pole chain; 36, backband hook; 37-40, breeching chains; 41-44, hame or shoulder chains; 45-47, crupper chain, D and hook; 48-49, backband ends; 50-53, bellyband ends; 54-55, trace ends; 56, wagon lock chain; 57, loom chain; 58, trace end; 59, watering chain; 60, check chain; 61, spring hook.

chain, on the other hand, became work-hardened very quickly and had to be annealed every few months in order to restore its physical properties. Compared to the modern product, it was not nearly as strong in relation to its weight.

The manufacture of modern chain is a highly technical and competitive process and firms that develop new techniques and machinery are careful to keep any successful innovations to themselves.

The traditional trade formed an important, if overlooked, part of Britain's industrial heritage and modern industry owes a debt to the sweat, skill and courage of the hand chainsmiths.

The most important area manufacturing wrought iron chain was undoubtedly that part of the industrial West Midlands of England known as the Black Country. Large chainworks also existed in the north-east of England at Gateshead, Newcastle upon Tyne and Sunderland and also at Saltney in Cheshire, Pontypridd in South Wales and Greenock in Scotland.

THE HISTORY OF IRON CHAIN

The history of the trade of chainmaking is in many respects obscure. Compared with other industries such as ironmaking, mining or engineering it was very small and therefore did not merit much attention from contemporary writers and historians. Furthermore, a large part of the trade, that of light chainmaking, was carried out in small domestic workshops by illiterate workers who kept no records.

However, in the early days the trade had much in common with that of the jobbing blacksmith. Specialised tools and techniques were developed on a very individualistic basis but once established remained unchanged until the end of hand chainmaking in the 1970s.

One part of the trade that was of great economic importance and was therefore documented was the manufacture of chain cable for the shipping industry. The first recorded patent for chain cables was taken out in 1634 by a Northumbrian blacksmith, Phillip White. From this date the use of iron chains for mooring cables can be traced.

Before the invention of iron cables the accepted way to moor a ship was with hempen ropes, which were easily damaged and were very limited as to the weight of ships they could safely hold. The first recorded instance of a ship with a chain cable was the 221 ton *Ann and Isabella,* built at Berwick-upon-Tweed in 1808. Her cable was made by a blacksmith, Robert Flinn, at his shop in Bell Street, North Shields.

The size of a piece of chain was stated as the measurement of the diameter of the iron rod that it was constructed from. The largest size of hemp cable in use was about 25 inches (634 mm) in circumference and weighed 6 tons. By 1847 the largest size of iron cable in use was $2\frac{1}{4}$ inches (57 mm) and this cost twenty per cent less to make than an equivalent in hemp. Before iron cables, a large ship in the Royal Navy would have had ten or eleven hemp cables. To replace these, four chain cables were thought to be sufficient.

One person who took a particular interest in iron cables was Samuel Brown, a lieutenant in the Royal Navy. In 1808 Brown took out a patent for cables made from twisted links. He made great efforts to get chain cables generally accepted and continued to advocate twisted links until about 1813. The disadvantage of Brown's twisted links with their pointed studs was that the cable was easily damaged under strain. A broad-studded untwisted cable patented in 1813 by a London merchant, Thomas Brunton, when tested against Brown's cable was reported to have 'torn Brown's links assunder'. This caused the navy to abandon the twisted link in favour of Brunton's design.

By 1820 small chainmaking had been established as a thriving industry in the Black Country for some time. This was probably because abundant supplies were available of good quality wrought iron and coke breeze for the hearths and because the local population was already skilled in the working of iron.

It was the firm of Hingley's which

A lady chainmaker photographed in July 1980. Preformed mild steel chain is automatically fed into her butt resistance welding machine. Electrodes press down on either side of the gap left in the link by the forming machine and the current fed generates heat at the high resistance point created by the gap itself. When the metal becomes hot enough, upsetting tools forge the butted ends together.

7

brought cable making to the area. In 1820 they undertook to make a 1½ inch (38 mm) chain for a Liverpool shipowner. This was a very large job for the time as no one in the district had made or even seen a chain of this size. However, after a few trial efforts the chainmakers, each with two strikers and two boys blowing the bellows, made the chain in 15 fathom (27.4 m) lengths. The links were end-welded and made of best Staffordshire iron. Cast iron studs were inserted in each link and the completed chain was so remarkable for its day that people came from miles around to see it. A feast and a day's holiday were given to celebrate its completion.

The success of this venture encouraged many others in the area to begin manufacturing chain cable. Noah Hingley's works grew from a small chainshop to an anchor works, and later ironworks, blast furnaces and collieries were added. By 1884 three thousand people were employed at Hingley's and the making of chain cables and anchors had become one of the biggest of the Staffordshire trades.

The growth of the hand chainmaking trade was to continue until the advent of the electric chain welding machine in the early twentieth century. The last full-time production of chain by hand in the Black Country ceased in 1975. The traditional trade had been kept alive by a handful of firms against the competition of the machine. A report in the *Financial Times* of December 1953 states that there were not more than a thousand iron chain workers left, spread over thirty-five firms, most of them very small. Compare this with 1896, when in the Cradley Heath district alone 1,000 tons of chain, from huge 4 inch (101 mm) mooring cables down to number sixteen on the wire gauge, were made each week by hand.

The arguments in favour of iron cable against steel and vice versa were continually aired. Wrought iron was said to have a longer life than steel, better shock-resisting properties and longer resistance to corrosion and to be easier to repair.

By the 1950s it was reported that few boys were entering the trade. This may have been because the work was felt to be too hard or because there was no confidence in the security of the job. The difficulty in obtaining suitable materials, the production of cheaper and better steel for the electric machines and the cessation of gas coke production were all factors which contributed towards the eventual decline of the traditional industry.

Several of the old buildings have been preserved by organisations such as the Black Country Museum, near Dudley (West Midlands) and Avoncroft Museum of Buildings, near Bromsgrove (Hereford and Worcester).

A Noah Hingley big chain gang at work on the anchor chain for the ill-fated 'Titanic'. The 'Titanic' struck an iceberg on 14th April 1912, during her maiden voyage. She sank with the loss of 1,600 lives.

ABOVE: *One of the more unusual maritime uses of chain, seen at Plymouth. The Torpoint ferry hauls itself along two lengths of chain which have been laid across the river. This technique enables the ferry to make a crossing unaffected by the push of current or tide.*

BELOW: *The chains for the ferry sustain wear and have to be replaced periodically. The new sets can be seen in the background vanishing into the water.*

ABOVE: *'The Glede Ovens', one of a series of Black Country industrial scenes etched by R. S. Chattock in 1872. Breeze or gledes was obtained by burning small pieces of coal in a dome-shaped oven until 'all smoke disappeared'. After removal of the breeze enough residual heat remained in the oven to ignite a fresh charge of coal.*

BELOW LEFT: *Brown's twisted links with their various forms of stud as illustrated in a book about chain cable published in 1884.*

BELOW RIGHT: *Domestic chainmaker's workshop in Cradley at the end of the nineteenth century.*

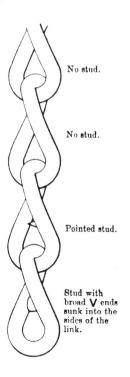

No stud.

No stud.

Pointed stud.

Stud with broad **V** ends sunk into the sides of the link.

A group of chainmakers outside the Cradley Chain Company works in the 1930s. Fourth from the left is Clarry Johnson, a chainmaker since he left school at the age of fourteen. Clarry has been most helpful to both the Black Country Museum and Avoncroft Museum of Buildings in their efforts to document and preserve the skills of the hand chainmaker for future generations to see.

WORKING CONDITIONS

Robert Sherard, who visited Cradley Heath in 1896, writing later in a popular magazine, described the town in harsh terms: 'It is frankly an industrial town, a town of the Black Country, where, in smoke and soot and mud, men and women earn their bread with the abundant sweat not of their brows alone; a terrible ugly and depressing town . . . one expects to find misery here.'

Nineteenth-century accounts of the appalling conditions and poor pay of the chainmakers are frequent and their work was often described in terms of slavery. Robert Blatchford, a radical journalist, wrote in 1899 of a visit to the chainshops of the Black Country. He described seeing makers of heavy chain — 'worn out old men of thirty-five' — and spoke of the men and women of Cradley being 'literally

worked to death for a living that no gentleman would offer his dogs'. His view of Cradley Heath agreed with Sherard's: 'a squalid and hideous place, ill-lighted and unpaved . . . the paths and roads heel-deep in mire.'

In workshops large and small all over the area men and women could be seen slaving away at their hearths making chain of all kinds, from huge 4 inch (101 mm) mooring cables to rigging chains, crane cables, mining cables, cart and plough traces, halters, cow ties and dog chains.

The bulk of Victorian criticism was reserved for the conditions experienced by the women and children in the trade. There is no doubt that they suffered intolerable hardships in order to scrape a bare existence. Robert Sherard interviewed several of these poor unfortunates on his journey

ABOVE: *The title page to Robert H. Sherard's article in Pearson's Magazine about the chainmakers of Cradley Heath.*

BELOW: *Domestic chainmakers' workshops in Cradley at the end of the nineteenth century.*

LEFT: *An illustration from Robert Sherard's article, showing a girl working a single bellows. Children were also employed to blow several pairs of bellows linked to a single rocker beam, to fill the hearths with breeze and to fetch jugs of beer for the chainmakers.*

RIGHT: *Interior of a Cradley chainshop about 1900. The largest size of chain normally made by women was known as 'bare 3/8'. A good woman working hard could make about $2\frac{1}{2}$ hundredweight (127 kg) of this size of chain per week.*

through the chainmaking area. One woman he spoke to worked at making heavy chain at 5s 4d per hundredweight (50.8 kg). By working a twelve-hour day she could make about $1\frac{1}{2}$ hundredweight (76.2 kg) each week. None of her family had 'more than he stood up in'. Her children 'had been weaned on sop', a concoction of bread and hot water flavoured with the drippings of the teapot, which they apparently relished. 'If them's got a basin of sop, them's as proud as if them's got a beefsteak.'

Another woman chainmaker he met gave him details of the birth of her 'little Johnny', born on 9th November 1895. His mother had worked until 5 pm on that day and then gone home because she had her household cleaning to do. Johnny was born at a quarter past seven that evening.

It was a common sight to see young children playing amongst the sparks or babies being rocked to sleep on the top of a pair of bellows while their mothers worked their iron into links.

Instances of exploitation abounded. For example, for forging a dog chain complete with its ring and swivel it was recorded that a woman was paid only three farthings. By working ten hours each day she could 'manage six chains in the day'. The dog chain apparently cost 1s 6d to buy from a retailer.

People known as 'foggers' flourished at the expense of the chainmakers. These merchants or middlemen bought the products of the chainmakers at one price and sold them at a much higher one. Sherard tells of a woman who received 2s 10d for every hundredweight of chain that she made. The fogger, in this case also a woman, then sold the chain for 5s 4d. Before government legislation in the form of the Truck Acts the chainmaker may have been paid not in cash but in the form of tokens. These tokens were only redeemable for goods and groceries at the fogger's own store. It was common practice to raise the price of such goods by as much as thirty per cent.

Sherard's description of the fogger sums her up very neatly: 'she has never forged a link of chain in her life and gets a good living . . . She is but one of a numerous class of human leeches fast to a gangrened sore.'

By 1904 Parliament had passed legislation to prevent more than twelve

hours being worked in every twenty-four, but little else had changed. At this time a woman chainmaker was paid 9s 6d for every hundredweight (50.8 kg) of $\frac{1}{8}$ inch (3 mm) chain that she made. For this she had to make 9,600 links. 1 hundredweight of iron contained about 600 feet (182.8 m) of $\frac{1}{8}$ inch rod and each foot (304 mm) was sufficient for sixteen links. The iron was supplied by the contractor and if the requisite number of links per hundredweight were not returned then a deduction in payment was made.

Sam Bloomer tommying a link at Noah Bloomer's of Quarry Bank in the early 1970s. Bloomer's was probably the last firm in England to make chain the traditional way. They closed their chainmaking operations in 1975.

ABOVE: *This woman, who had been making chain for fifty-six years, worked in a small one-hearth workshop in Hall Street, Old Hill. The bellows were operated by means of a wooden handle known as the 'rock'. The sieve hanging on the wall was used when washing dirt from the breeze.*

BELOW: *A restored chainshop with attached 'one up and one down' cottage, at Mushroom Green in the Black Country.*

ABOVE: *One of the chainshops of the former Cradley firm of Jones and Lloyd. The firm was established by Joseph and William Rock in 1837 but changed to Jones and Lloyd in 1867. Their trade card listed them as being 'manufacturers of colliery lashing chains, pit cage chains, coal cutter chains, incline and crane chains, drawbars, couplings and colliery tub ironwork, and cables and anchors to Lloyds requirements'. The firm closed in 1969 but one of their purpose-built workshops, the fourteen-hearth Scotia Works, was saved from destruction by being dismantled and later reconstructed at Avoncroft Museum of Buildings. The unglazed barred windows with wooden shutters and the ventilators on the roof are typical features of nineteenth-century chainshops.*

BELOW: *The interior of Jones and Lloyd's chainshop at Avoncroft Museum of Buildings.*

The chainmaking demonstrator at the Black Country Museum. The reconstructed chainshop there is based on the layout of the old Cruddas Chain Yard of Cradley Heath.

TOP LEFT: *The link-bending machine at Noah Hingley's at the end of the nineteenth century. Large diameter bars, which were intended to be side-welded into links, were first heated in a coal-fired reverberatory furnace and then bent into link shape on this type of machine.*

BOTTOM FAR LEFT: *The machine-bent links were reheated in another furnace and hooked out as required. One of the chainmaking team would then drag the hot link over to the hearth and lift it, scarfed ends uppermost, on to the stake. A sledge hammer with a tapered end, the 'opener', was used next to open up the scarfs. Once the scarfs were opened up the link was thrust into the hearth and when hot enough brought out, placed on the stake and the previously welded link was threaded on to it. The scarfed ends were then closed with a 'johnny', a two-handled hammer weighing about 28 pounds (12.7 kg).*

BOTTOM NEAR LEFT: *The link was returned to the fire and brought to a welding heat. Once at the required temperature, the link was brought swiftly on to the stake and a hollow-faced tool, the 'squabber', was placed over the scarf and struck with the johnny. In this way half of the weld was made. The link had to be returned to the fire for the other half to be completed in the same way as before. During the welding process a little silver sand was sometimes used as a flux.*

ABOVE: *Finally a stud of the appropriate size was inserted and the sides were set down to hold it firmly. A hollow-faced tool is run over the side to prevent the striking hammer from marking the link.*

SHUTTING CHAIN

'If you asked a chainmaker how many links he'd made, he might say: "Well, I've shut eighty before breakfast and I've shut sixty since." *Shut*, see — never *welded.*' So said Clarry Johnson, chainmaker.

The making of chain by hand can be roughly divided into three sections: heavy, medium and light.

Heavy chainmaking, that is chain from 1 inch (25 mm) diameter upwards, involved a team of men. The team consisted of a chainmaker and several strikers. The number of men needed as strikers was determined by the size of chain being worked. Chain from about 2 inches (50 mm) upwards was welded on the side, although occasionally $1\frac{3}{4}$ inch (44 mm) chain was also made in this way.

Heavy chainmaking was a job organised into factories and the work was done on a

ABOVE: *This photograph, taken in the 1950s, shows the start of the sequence for making stud link on a dolly with two strikers. To speed things up cropped bars of iron were preheated above the hearth on a sloping rack and were lifted from here with a pair of hollow bits and thrust into the heart of the fire as required, so allowing the next bar to roll down over the heat. The long-handled shovel lying across the breeze was called a 'scoven' and was used to move the breeze around the hearth. The bottle on the back of the hearth probably contained cold tea, which few chainmakers would be without.*
TOP RIGHT: *Once the link had been scarfed out and the ends laid over, it was brought up to a welding heat and struck by the three men in turn. The skill required to keep each blow in time with the others must have been considerable.*
BOTTOM RIGHT: *After the link had been 'shut' the dolly arm was flipped over and while the two strikers hit the top of the dolly the chainmaker manipulated the link on the point. This ensured that the hammer marks caused at the welding stage were smoothed off.*

piecework system. The chainmaker was paid by the firm on a weight basis. If he needed help in the form of strikers, the chainmaker organised the men and paid them from his own wages. This system of subcontracting was known as the *butty*.

Medium chainmaking was the job of one man, who used a foot-operated treadle hammer, the *tommy*, to smooth off and consolidate the weld. This section of the trade was carried out both in factory shops, usually long narrow buildings with hearths down each side, and in smaller domestic workshops which contained only one or two hearths. Chains from about $\frac{1}{2}$ inch (12 mm) to 1 inch (25 mm) were made in this way.

Light chainmaking was almost exclusively carried out in small domestic workshops. The coke-fired hearth was housed in a small building adjoining the worker's house. Light chain, up to $\frac{3}{8}$ inch (9.5 mm) in size, was usually the work of women. They were supplied with iron rods

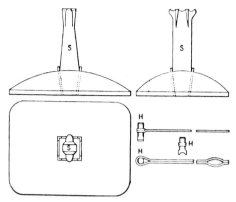

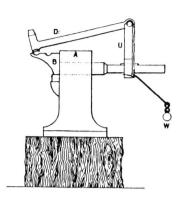

ABOVE: *Diagrams of tools used in the heavy chain trade, from a book published in 1884. The left-hand sketch shows a stake (S) and hollow-faced tools used when side-welding. The right-hand sketch is of a dolly (D), bickiron (B) and anvil (A). The weight (W) was to prevent the dolly from bouncing when it was hit with the hand hammers.*

from 8 to 10 feet (2.4 to 3.0 m) in length, which they cut to a manageable length for working themselves. These *bundles* of iron weighed ½ hundredweight (25.4 kg). When the finished chain was weighed with a view to payment the same unit was again used, but in this instance a *bundle* weighed only 52 pounds (23.5 kg). The discrepancy was because of the allowance made for loss of weight due to *scaling*. The larger the diameter of the rod, the more metal flaked or scaled off when it was heated. The scaling allowance varied from place to place.

According to one of the last of the women chainmakers, Lucy Woodall, who worked as an outworker for several firms, 'If you were an outworker they used to allow you 8 pounds on a hundredweight for scaling off. Well, if you gained a pound they would pay you, but if you were a pound out, they would take it off you as well. But you'd allus got the scale off your links you know. Years gone by they used to clean the knives and forks with it, and the old enamel teapots. They'd come up as white as snow. They'd get a damp rag and dip it in the "slick" and rub it well. They even used to clean the lavatories with it.'

In all sections of the trade, speed was essential if a living wage was to be earned.

RIGHT: *A typical medium chainmaking block. The 'block' was the name given to the base into which the main tools were fixed. (1) Linkage rods. These lengths of iron rod with curved ends were used to connect the tommy to the spring pole and treadle. (2) The die. The size of the die varied with the size of iron being worked. When the treadle was being operated the die had to come down accurately over the point of the bickiron. The die shaped the outside of the weld and the bickiron the underside. (3) The tommy. This was the treadle-operated hammer, which pivoted on needle bearings between two uprights. Various sizes of die could be wedged in a square hole in the face of the tommy. (4) The stumps, the two solid uprights, usually of wood, set into the floor of the chainshop. The tommy pivoted between them. (5) The tommy arm. This was fixed firmly to the tommy with a U bolt. The linkage rod to the foot treadle was hooked over the end of this arm. (6) The slides. Held in four ring bolts, the slides could be knocked backward or forward with a hammer in order to adjust the position where the die came down over the bickiron. The die and bickiron had to 'work level and close' and gave better results after being worked in for some time. (7) The bender. Precut and heated bars of iron were levered into ninety degree bends in this ring before being knocked down into U shape. (8) The bickiron. This was a hollow-faced tool held fast in the anvil or stake. A set-off on the anvil allowed a wedge to be driven under the bickiron to hold it secure. The size of the point of the bickiron varied with the diameter of iron being worked. (9) The gauge. (10) The hardy. (11) The swedge. (See diagram of woman chainmaker's block on page 28.) (12) Treadle. The treadle controlled the tommy and was hooked up to the tommy arm when work began.*

22

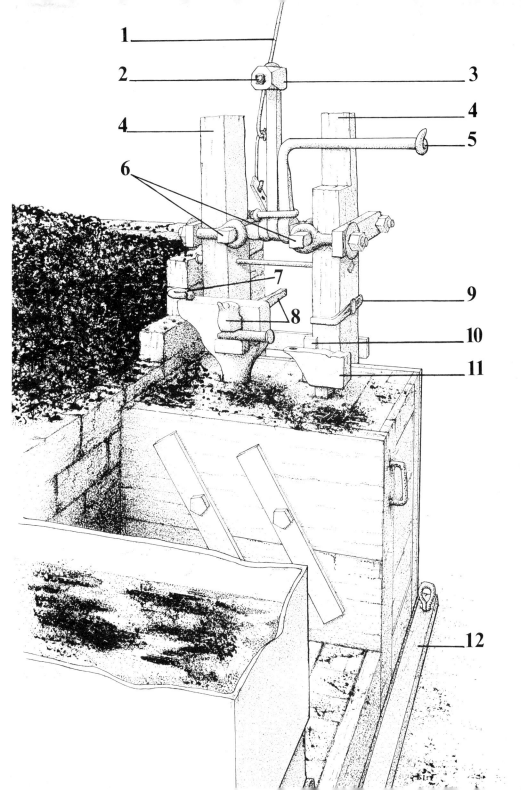

ABOVE: *The stages in making an end-welded link. The cold bar was cut on mechanical shears, then heated in the hearth and bent to a U shape. The ends were reheated and then 'scarfed out' or flattened. These scarfed ends were next bent one over the other on the point of the bickiron. After reheating to welding heat, about 1,300C (2,370F), which was judged by eye, the ends were 'shut' together using the hand hammer. A tommy or dolly was then used to smooth off and consolidate the weld. Chain from about 2 inches (50 mm) downwards was normally end-welded.*

The number of links a chainmaker could manufacture in a given period depended on several factors. These included his individual skill at the job, the size and quality of his iron and the quality of his fuel.

Particularly in the latter days of the trade fuel could be very poor and a chainmaker might have to stop after making ten links in order to clean the fire. With good fuel he might have been able to work solidly for one or two hours at a time.

Any impurities and dirt in the breeze formed into a treacly mass in front of and below the tue-iron. In this hot state it was known as *layter*. If any layter got between the ends of a link it prevented a good weld. When the fire was allowed to cool the layter solidified into a lump of clinker which could be levered out with a poker and discarded.

Working with good iron and fuel, chainmaker Clarry Johnson could make fifty or sixty $\frac{1}{2}$ inch (12 mm) links every hour. The larger the size of the iron, the longer it took to heat up and work into a link.

The working day for the chainmakers began at about 5 am and ended when a sufficient quota of work had been completed, usually at midday. The most common theory put forward as to the reason for this pattern of work was that the chainmakers wished to get their time in on the hearth before the day became too hot. There is doubt about the truth of this because the same hours were worked in winter and summer.

This early start to the day was not without its problems. Clarry Johnson recalled that Jones and Lloyd received a complaint from nearby householders about noise. However, it was not the constant banging of the tommy hammers that had caused the disturbance; presumably the neighbourhood had grown used to this. It was the chainmakers' habit of singing while they worked that was the cause of the annoyance.

RIGHT: *A typical hearth for medium-size chain. (1) Spring pole. This was a long, strong wooden pole fixed in the roof of the chainshop. It lifted the tommy back to its upright position after it had been brought down with the foot treadle. (2) Sweat cloth. A piece of absorbent cloth was hung on a hook so as to be within easy reach of the chainmaker, who would periodically wipe the sweat from his face with it. (3) Throw pipe. Steam from the water-cooled tue-iron rose up this pipe. The steam condensed at the top and the water dropped back into the back bosh. (4) The shed. A metal sheet was hung in front of the fire to shield the chainmaker from heat, glare and spitting coke. (5) Breeze, the small pieces of coke normally used as fuel for chainmaking. (6) The back bosh. The back or hearth bosh contained the reservoir of cooling water for the tue-iron. (7) The cold bosh. This contained the water to cool off the tongs. The chainmaker would also dip his arms in the water periodically and splash it up on to the shed in order to cool it and himself down. (8) The treadle. This was operated by the chainmaker's right foot to bring down the tommy.*

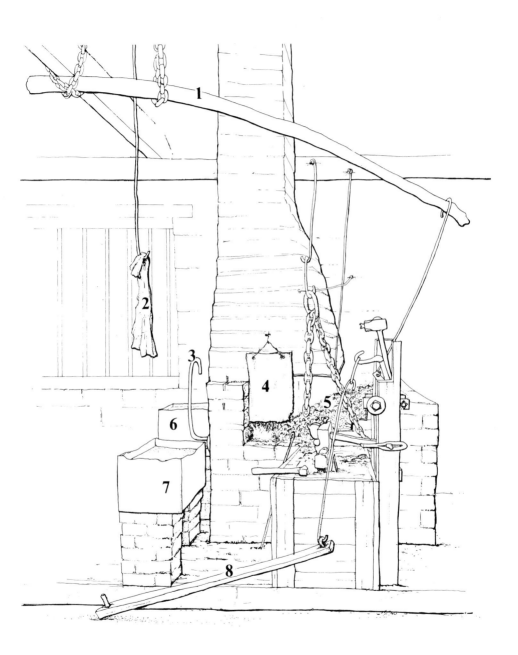

Tommying a link on the demonstration hearth at Avoncroft Museum's chainshop. In order to smooth off the link the chainmaker had to bring down the treadle in a series of rhythmic blows while turning the link on the point of the bickiron. The shutters on the barred windows of the chainshop would normally have been kept open for ventilation, but they are seen closed here to assist photography.

LEFT: *Clarry Johnson in his working clothes. His vest or 'gansey', reinforced with a piece of cotton duck at the front, shows signs of the sparks or 'flashes' that have shot off the links as he worked. The protective canvas apron around his waist and the sweatcloth, draped here around his neck, were also essential items. When work stopped, a woollen jumper and a muffler were quickly to hand, to prevent chills.*

BELOW: *A set of chainmaker's tongs used for making $\frac{1}{2}$ inch (12 mm) chain. The top two pairs of 'nipple tongs' were used to hold the link sideways on when scarfing, laying over, welding and tommying. The central two pairs of 'hollow bits' held the bars endways on while they were heated at the initial stages. The bottom pair of 'benders' were used to crank the hot bar into a ninety degree bend, before knocking it down into a full U shape with the hand hammer.*

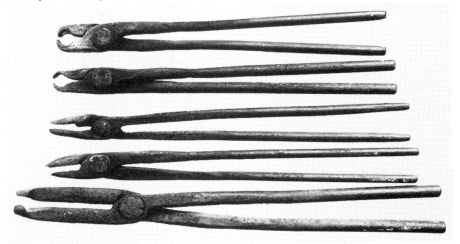

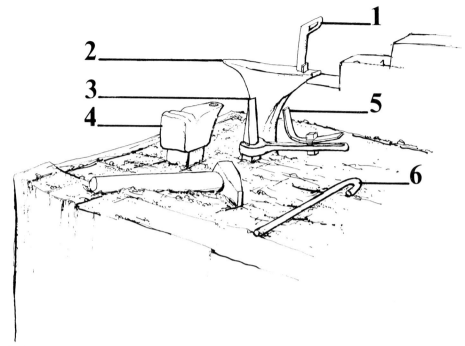

ABOVE: *A woman chainmaker's block. (1) The twister. Twisted chain was made by inserting hot links in this tool and levering them over ninety degrees. (2) The bikkon. This corresponded with the men chainmakers' bickiron. The ends of the U-shaped links were bent over on it in a similar way. (3) The hardy. The hardy or cutter was used to sever lengths of hot rod. (4) The swedge. This small anvil was used when bending the rod into a U shape. (5) The gauge. This could be adjusted backward or forward according to the length of rod required to be severed on the hardy. (6) The dog. The curved end of the dog was slipped over the jaws of the tongs when twisting chain in order to prevent damage to them and also to give leverage. Very small chain could be twisted without the dog.*

LEFT: *Women chainmakers formed the first part of their links 'off the rod'. The end of the hot rod was pushed up against the gauge and the section over the hardy was struck with the hammer.*

The partially severed section was then formed into a ninety degree bend.

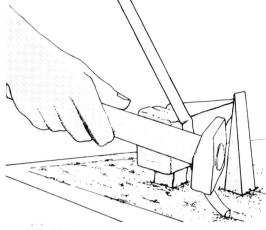

The bent rod was then knocked down into a full U shape.

Once formed, the U could be easily twisted off the length of rod and returned to the hearth. Small chain did not need to have the ends scarfed before welding; they were simply 'jumped' together. The weld was then smoothed off with strokes of the hand hammer.

SPECIAL TREBLE BEST LOADING CHAIN

of the Celebrated J  L Brand.

"THE CHAIN THAT DOES NOT BREAK."

This is a piece of our ⅜ in. exact size chain, tested to destruction, breaking at **8,850lbs.** See how the links have stretched before breaking.

Note the great strength of these links at the weld. The weld is wrapped well round the link, thus increasing the resistance to sudden strains or jerks, and giving a reliability which is conspicuously absent in other makes of logging chains, which invariably break at their weakest part—the weld. By our method the thickening of the weld is carried to such a point as to make it actually the strongest portion of the link.

GUARANTEE. We guarantee that this chain is made throughout of the finest "Refined" Material obtainable, and that the greatest care and the strictest supervision are exercised to ensure perfect welding.

Any chain which breaks owing to faulty material or defective welding will be immediately replaced.

Allow us to convince you of the superiority of this chain over every other make by sending you a supply. All sizes in stock.

$\frac{9}{32}$ $\frac{10}{32}$ $\frac{11}{32}$ $\frac{3}{8}$ ins. dia.

Prices per cwt.

ABOVE: *Part of Jones and Lloyd's publicity material, promising the hand-made chain that did not break.*

BELOW: *These were the stamps that were applied to lengths of chain at the Sunderland Proving House in 1881. One link in every 5 fathoms (9.1 m) had to be stamped.*

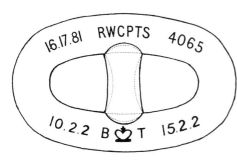

16 =	No. of License of Breaking Machine.
17 =	„ „ Tensile Machine.
81 =	Year in which the License was granted.
RWCPTS =	River Wear Commission Public Trust, Sunderland.
4065 =	No. of Certificate.
10.2.2 =	Tensile Strain, viz.:—10 tons 2 cwt. 2 qrs.
B ♛ T =	Board of Trade.
15.2.2 =	Breaking Strain, viz.:—15 tons 2 cwt. 2 qrs.

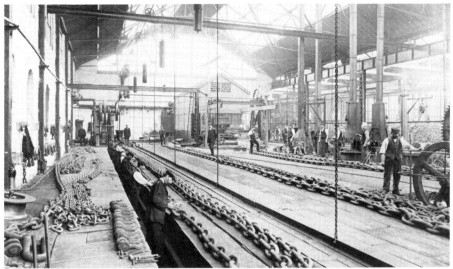

A proving house in the Black Country in 1900.

TESTING CHAIN

The importance of testing a length of chain to ensure its suitability and strength for a particular job was realised early in the history of the trade. In 1812 Samuel Brown had a testing machine constructed at his chainworks in London. This enabled him to find out where defects in material, construction and workmanship lay and thereby gradually to improve the quality of his cables. He also used his machine to test the mechanical properties of the iron he was supplied with. However, it was not until 1846 that the Rules of Lloyd's Shipping Register made it their surveyor's duty to see that ship's cables had been tested and that the strain applied had been stamped on each length.

Even so, the quality and therefore the safety of these early chain cables varied enormously and so did the tests that were applied to them. In 1864 the first Act of Parliament regulating the proving, testing and sale of chain cables and anchors was passed. The Act stated: 'from and after the first day of July 1865 it shall not be lawful for any maker of or dealer in chain cables or anchors to sell or contract to sell for the use of any vessel any chain cable whatever or any anchor exceeding in weight 168 pounds unless such chain cable or anchor shall have been previously tested and duly stamped in accordance with the provisions of this Act.' The penalty for contravening this was a fine of up to £50.

In later years several amendments were made but the basic requirements of tensile and breaking strain tests remained unchanged.

According to the amended Act of 1871 cables were to be tested as follows: three links were to be taken from every 15 fathoms (27.4 m) and subjected to the appropriate breaking strain; if these links failed a second three links were cut and tested in the same way; if either of the two pieces withstood the breaking strain, the remaining links from the 15 fathoms were subjected to the correct tensile strain; cable that withstood the strain was stamped 'as proved'.

Modern regulations governing the testing and subsequent use of chain cables and chains are strict. This is a great advance from the situation that existed in the nineteenth century, at the height of hand-made chain production.

BIBLIOGRAPHY

Barnsley, P. 'An Esteemed Black Country Lady'. *The Black Countryman* magazine, volume 4, number 1.
Burnett, J. *Nailmakers and Small Chainmakers*. Board of Trade Report, 1888.
Comer, D. *Inside Industry's Vital Link*. Parsons Chain Company, 1980.
CoSIRA. *The Blacksmith's Craft*. CoSIRA, 1976.
Cossons, N. *The BP Book of Industrial Archaeology*. David and Charles, 1975.
Gale, W. K. V. *Iron and Steel*. David and Charles, 1977.
Gale, W. K. V. 'Hand Wrought Chains'. *Newcomen Society Records* volume XXIX, 1955.
Moss, R. *Mushroom Green Chainshop*. The Black Country Society, 1977.
Sherard, R. H. 'The White Slaves of England'. *Pearsons Magazine*, 1896.
Smith, R. M. *Sweated Industries*. A Handbook of the Daily News Exhibition, 1906.
Traill, T. *Chain Cables and Chains*. Crosby Lockwood and Company, 1874.

PLACES TO VISIT

Avoncroft Museum of Buildings, Stoke Heath, Bromsgrove, Hereford and Worcester. Telephone: Bromsgrove (0527) 31363. Re-erected factory chainshop from Cradley.
North of England Open Air Museum, Beamish Hall, Stanley, County Durham. Telephone: Stanley (0207) 31811. Small display on chainmaking. Chainmaker's tools in store for future reconstruction of workshop.
Black Country Museum, Tipton Road, Dudley, West Midlands. Telephone: 021-557 9643. Re-erected and reconstructed chainshops with regular demonstrations.
Mushroom Green Chainshop, near Dudley, West Midlands. Restored chainshop with attached cottage. Information from the Black Country Museum or the Black Country Society, 49 Victoria Road, Tipton, West Midlands.

ACKNOWLEDGEMENTS

Illustrations are acknowledged as follows: Birmingham Post and Mail, page 1; Charles Fogg, pages 2, 7, 9 (both), 12 (top), 13 (top), 15 (bottom), 16 (both), 17, 23, 24, 25, 26, 27 (bottom), 28 (both), 29 (all); Black Country Museum, pages 3, 10 (top), 18 (top), 19, 31; Avoncroft Museum of Buildings, pages 4, 5, 14, 30 (top); Birmingham Reference Library, page 8; Thomas Traill, pages 10 (bottom left), 22, 30 (bottom); Birmingham City Museum, pages 10 (bottom right), 12 (bottom), 13 (bottom); Clarry Johnson, pages 11, 32; W. K. V. Gale, pages 15 (top), 18 (bottom two), 20, 21 (both); Janine Wiedel, page 27 (top).

Special thanks are due to Jenny Costigan, Keith Gale, Stuart Holm, Clarry Johnson and Lucy Woodall.

The firm of Henry Wood and Company was established in 1780 at Stourbridge. The works at Saltney were built in 1847.

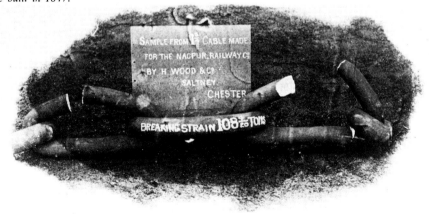